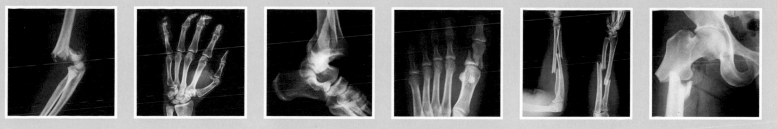

LIFE
SUPPORT

THOMAS CANAVAN

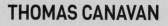

FRANKLIN WATTS
LONDON • SYDNEY

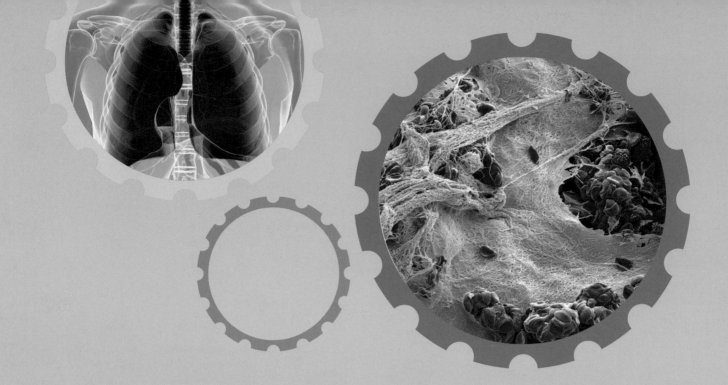

First published in 2015 by Franklin Watts

Copyright © Arcturus Holdings Limited

Franklin Watts
338 Euston Road
London NW1 3BH

Franklin Watts Australia
Level 17/207 Kent Street, Sydney NSW 2000

Produced by Arcturus Publishing Limited,
26/27 Bickels Yard, 151–153 Bermondsey Street, London SE1 3HA

Author: Thomas Canavan
Editors: Joe Harris, Joe Fullman, Nicola Barber and Sam Williams
Designer: Elaine Wilkinson
Original design concept and cover design: Notion Design

Picture Credits:
Key: b-bottom, m-middle, l-left, r-right, t-top
All images courtesy of Shutterstock, apart from: Corbis: p5 bl. Lee Montgomery and Anne Sharp: back cover, p30, p31.
Science Photo Library: p2 r, p3 tr, p16 l, p21 bl (John Bavosi), p21 br,
p17 t (Laboratory of Molecular Biology/MRC), p22 l (Medical RF.com).

A CIP catalogue for this book is available from the British Library.

Dewey Decimal Classification Number: 612.17

ISBN: 978 1 4451 4338 5

Printed in China

Franklin Watts is a division of Hachette Children's Books, an Hachette UK company.
www.hachette.co.uk

SL004510UK

Supplier: 13, Date 0315, Print run 3892

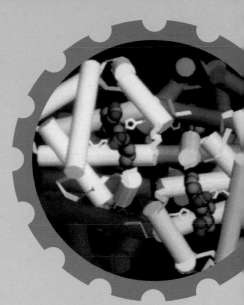

CONTENTS

LIFE SUPPORT 04

HAVE A HEART 06

ROUND AND ROUND 08

TAKE CARE OF YOUR HEART 10

A BREATH OF FRESH AIR 12

SPEAK OUT! 14

HEART AND LUNG FACTS 16

TESTING YOUR LIMITS 18

JACK OF ALL TRADES 20

GET THE MESSAGE? 22

DID YOU KNOW? 24

FREQUENTLY ASKED QUESTIONS 26

SYSTEMS OF THE BODY 28

GLOSSARY 30

FURTHER READING 31

INDEX 32

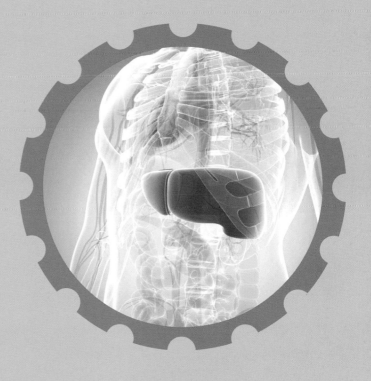

LIFE SUPPORT

Your lungs and heart are always working, even while you sleep. Your lungs take in a gas called oxygen from the air. Meanwhile, your heart pumps blood to every part of your body. That blood contains oyxgen which it gets from your lungs. Without oxygen, your body would not work properly.

Chilling Out

When you exercise, your lungs and heart get to work immediately. You breathe harder and your heart beats much faster. This is so that more oxygen can reach your muscles to keep your body moving. As you get fitter, your body starts to work much harder and for longer.

WORKING OUT

FREAKING OUT

A shock or a fright can make you breathe quicker and your heart beat faster. This 'fight or flight' response is your body's way of helping you to survive scary situations by preparing you for intense physical action. So, when you're afraid, your lungs take in air faster to supply your blood with oxygen, and your heart beats faster so it can pump more blood to your muscles.

Heart

HAVE A HEART

Your heart is about the size of your fist and it has a very important job to do. It pumps blood that's full of oxygen hard and fast enough to reach every part of your body. Nothing would work without that oxygen-rich blood, so your heart really is an important organ.

BODY PUMP

Your heart sits in the middle of your chest, protected by your ribs. It is close to your lungs and works like a pump. Before each heartbeat, your heart fills up with blood. Then, it squeezes sharply – which is the beat – to send blood squirting away to other parts of your body. Did you know your heart beats about 100,000 times in one day and about 35 million times in a year. That's pretty amazing!

DISTANT DRUMS

You can feel your heartbeat by putting your hand on your chest. But the beats are strong enough to be felt well away from your heart. You can feel them by checking your pulse. Place your fingers just above one of your larger arteries (which carry blood from the heart). One pulse is on the side of your neck. Another is on the inside of your wrist.

ACTIVITY

Ask a friend to put their two first fingers lightly down on your inner wrist. When they feel a pulse, ask them to count it while you time them for 15 seconds. Multiply the result by four to get your pulse rate (beats per minute).

HEART AT WORK

Your heart is made up of four chambers: left atrium, right atrium, left ventricle and right ventricle. The right side receives deoxygenated blood (blood in which the oxygen has been used up) from the body and sends it to the lungs, where oxygen is added. The left side takes the blood from the lungs and pumps it to the rest of your body. Deoxygenated blood arrives at the heart through blood vessels called veins, while oxygenated blood leaves the heart through blood vessels called arteries. Valves in the heart stop blood from flowing in the wrong direction.

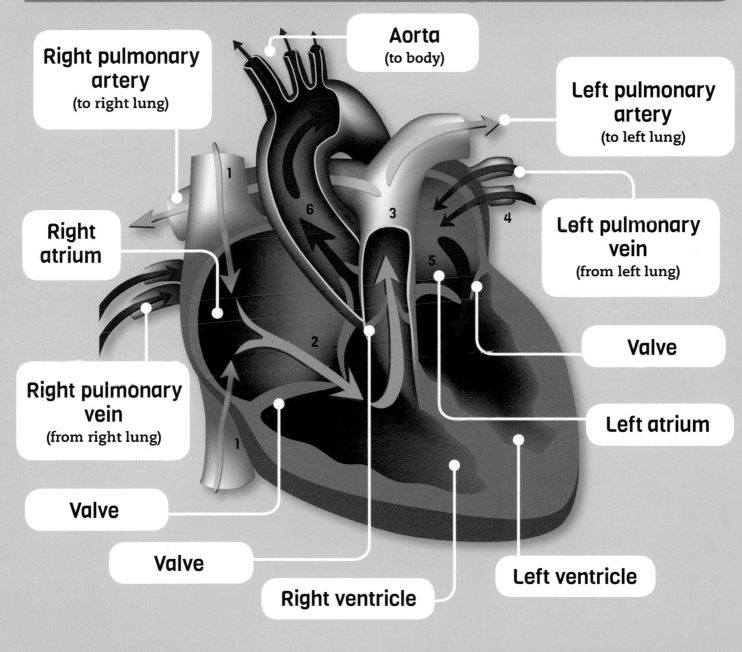

Right pulmonary artery
(to right lung)

Aorta
(to body)

Left pulmonary artery
(to left lung)

Right atrium

Left pulmonary vein
(from left lung)

Right pulmonary vein
(from right lung)

Valve

Left atrium

Valve

Valve

Left ventricle

Right ventricle

1 Blood from body into the heart
2 Blood from right atrium to right ventricle
3 Blood from right ventricle to lungs
4 Oxygen-rich blood from lungs into left atrium
5 Oxygen-rich blood into left ventricle
6 Oxygen-rich blood out to body

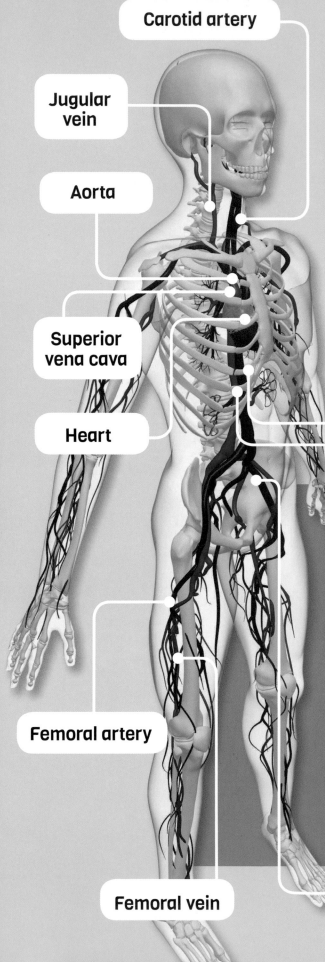

Carotid artery

Jugular vein

Aorta

Superior vena cava

Heart

Femoral artery

Femoral vein

Descending aorta

Inferior vena cava

Iliac artery

ROUND AND ROUND

Your heart and all the veins and arteries carrying blood are called the circulatory system. It works a lot like a delivery system. Your body needs oxygen and other ingredients just to keep working. So, your heart pumps out blood to all parts of your body. When it has made its deliveries, the blood returns to the heart to get more oxygen – and the cycle begins all over again.

IN THE LOOP

Your circulatory system carries blood loaded with oxygen and nutrients around your body. If you compare your circulatory system to a road network, the biggest and busiest routes are the arteries and veins. The aorta is the largest artery. The heart pumps oxygen-rich blood from the left ventricle through the aorta. The aorta divides and branches into smaller arteries – such as the carotid artery in the neck – which carry the blood to all parts of your body. After your body's cells have received the oxygen, it's the job of the veins to take your blood back to your heart. The biggest veins are the two that enter the heart. The superior vena cava carries blood from your arms and head. The inferior vena cava carries blood up from your lower body.

BRANCH LINES

Arteries and veins are connected by tiny tubes called capillaries. These are so thin that blood from the arteries passes through them easily. The blood cells release their oxygen to the surrounding body cells through the capillary wall. At the same time, they pick up waste from the body cells. The main type of waste is a gas called carbon dioxide. Then the blood travels into the veins, ready for transport back to the heart.

Blood from heart

Capillaries

Vein

Artery

Blood to heart

BLOOD CELLS

Your blood contains three main types of cell. Red blood cells collect oxygen from your lungs. This oxygen is packed into compartments inside the red blood cells, along with vitamins and other nutrients. White blood cells help your body to fight infection. Platelets are the smallest cells. Their job is to repair holes in the linings of blood vessels. They also help you to make a scab when you cut yourself. All the cells float inside a liquid called plasma.

The human body has about

100,000 km (60,000 miles)

of blood vessels – enough to go around the world about two and a half times!

TAKE CARE OF YOUR HEART

Your heart needs to be exercised regularly to stay healthy. It's not too hard to give it a gentle workout – after all, it beats more than 100,000 times every day and you don't need to do anything to make it work. Your body automatically produces a burst of electricity that triggers each of those heart beats.

HEALTHY HEART, HEALTHY YOU

Your heart may work automatically, but to keep a healthy heart, it's mostly up to you to make sure you don't make it struggle. For example, your heart is just the right size to pump your blood around your body. But if you put on too much weight, your heart can find the job much harder to do.

TAKE SOME EXERCISE

Regular exercise helps your heart stay healthy, and it keeps you fit. It also makes your heart stronger – it is a muscle, after all. If your heart has to struggle to pump blood around your body, then your muscles and other parts of your body, won't get enough oxygen. That means you'll have less energy, which is why people who are unfit get tired and out of breath very quickly.

Regular exercise helps strengthen your heart and improves circulation!

SMOKE SIGNALS

Smoking damages blood cells and causes a waxy substance to build up in the arteries. Over time, this substance hardens and makes it difficult for the blood to pass through the arteries. This can lead to heart disease, heart attacks and even heart failure.

RUN FOR YOUR LIFE

Running is a really simple exercise that increases your heart rate and helps you to stay healthy. You don't need any equipment and it's free!

EAT HEART-HEALTHY FOOD

Eating fresh vegetables and fruit in a balanced diet is good for you, as you body gets the nutrients it needs to operate smoothly. Also, fresh foods don't contain added ingredients that can cause trouble with your heart and blood vessels.

 ACTIVITY

You can demonstrate the strain blockages create for blood vessels. Stretch a long balloon and cut the closed tip. Slide one end over a garden hose, hold it and slowly turn the hose on. Water will come out of the other end just like a blood flow. Now pinch the far end. Water strains against the balloon just like blood that's been blocked.

SALTY SNACKS – GO EASY!

Too much salt can be bad for you. Eating too many salty snacks causes your body to hold on to more water. The extra liquid in your blood puts more pressure on the walls of the blood vessels and also on your heart.

A BREATH OF FRESH AIR

Your lungs make up one of the largest organs in your body. They work with your respiratory (breathing) system to allow you to take in fresh air. Although you can't see it, the air you breathe is made up of several gases. Oxygen is the most important gas because your body needs it for energy and growth.

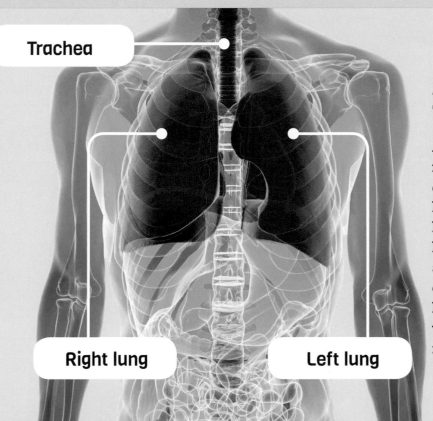

Trachea

Right lung

Left lung

A TRIP DOWN THE TRACHEA

As you breathe in, air travels from your mouth and nose down to your lungs. Both of your lungs do the same job, but your left lung is slightly smaller, to leave space for your heart. The air travels down your windpipe, called the trachea. The trachea is lined with tiny hairs called cilia which catch dust particles that may have floated in with the air.

BRANCHING OFF

When your trachea reaches your lungs, it divides into two tubes, called bronchi, which connect to the lungs. Here, they branch into smaller bronchi, which fork again into even smaller tubes, about the width of a human hair, called bronchioles. There are around 30,000 bronchioles in each of your lungs. They end in tiny air sacs, called alveoli. A single alveoli is called an alveolus.

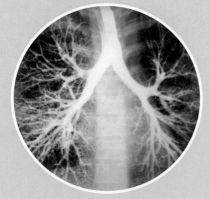

GAS EXCHANGE

The job of your respiratory system is to bring oxygen gas into your body and get rid of the waste, which is another gas called carbon dioxide. As you breathe in, oxygen passes through the walls of the alveoli into the blood cells in the capillaries. Once it's loaded with oxygen, the blood is ready to move on. But before it does, the blood cells release the waste carbon dioxide into the alveoli. Then, the process is reversed so that you breathe out the waste.

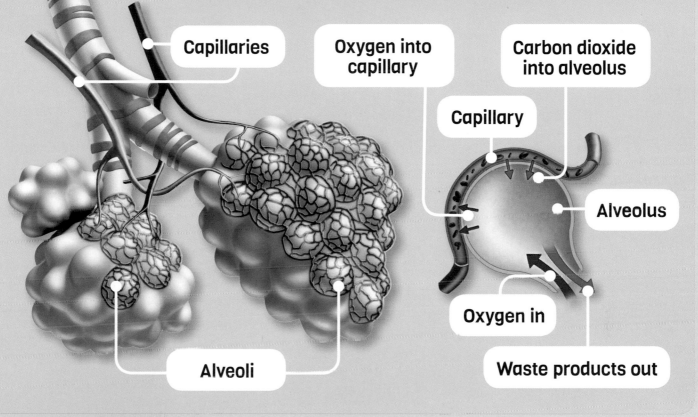

Bronchiole

Capillaries

Oxygen into capillary

Carbon dioxide into alveolus

Capillary

Alveolus

Oxygen in

Alveoli

Waste products out

STRAIGHT TO THE HEART

From the lungs, oxygen-rich blood heads straight to the heart through the pulmonary vein, ready to be pumped around the body. The movement of blood between the heart and the lungs is called pulmonary circulation.

If you spread out the 300 million alveoli in a pair of adult lungs, their surface area would be about as large as a tennis court!

SPEAK OUT!

One of the hardest-working muscles in your body is your diaphragm. It makes sure you breathe in air that's rich in oxygen, and breathe out air that's full of waste. That flow of air that comes out of you also creates the sounds you make to communicate – whether it's a hushed whisper, a loud shout or a happy song!

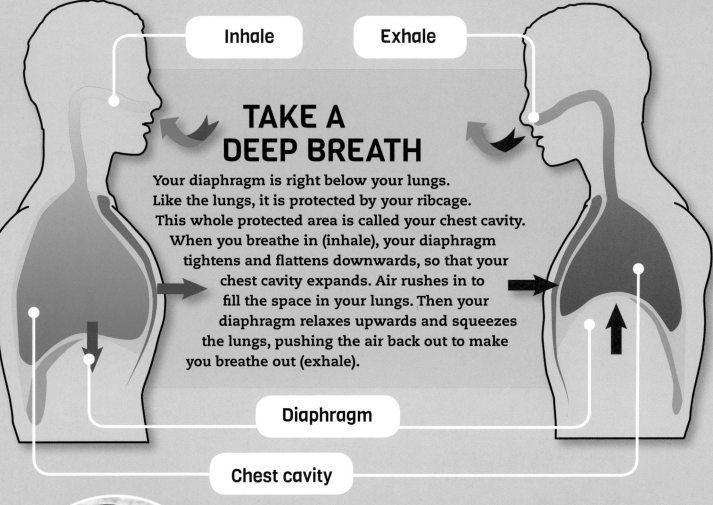

Inhale

Exhale

TAKE A DEEP BREATH

Your diaphragm is right below your lungs. Like the lungs, it is protected by your ribcage. This whole protected area is called your chest cavity. When you breathe in (inhale), your diaphragm tightens and flattens downwards, so that your chest cavity expands. Air rushes in to fill the space in your lungs. Then your diaphragm relaxes upwards and squeezes the lungs, pushing the air back out to make you breathe out (exhale).

Diaphragm

Chest cavity

OUT IT GOES

Breathing out is just as important as breathing in! Your body needs to get rid of carbon dioxide and other waste. If carbon dioxide builds up in your blood or lungs, it can affect your muscles and your breathing. You can hold your breath for a short time, but eventually your body forces you to breathe out!

SOMETHING TO SHOUT ABOUT

The sounds you make are created in the larynx, or voicebox, which sits at the top of your trachea (windpipe). When you talk, your vocal cords in your voicebox tighten up and move closer together. Air from the lungs is forced between them and this makes them move, or vibrate. This vibration produces the sound of your voice. Your tongue, lips and teeth help you to form this sound into words. As you grow older, your larynx gets bigger and this makes your voice deepen.

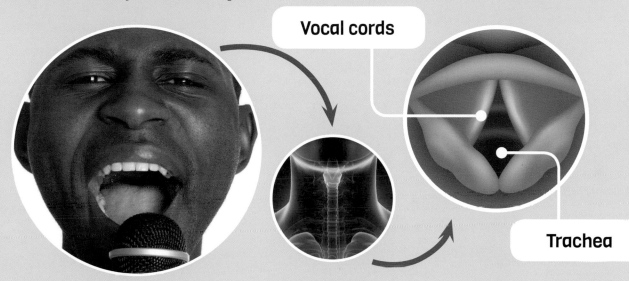

Vocal cords

Trachea

ACTIVITY

Yawning is contagious! Sit down with a friend and then both try and relax. Then, ask your friend to yawn. You'll soon find yourself joining in as well! A yawn is an exercise for your lungs because it stretches them and keeps them fit.

In 1994, Annalisa Flanagan won a shouting contest and broke the world record for the loudest voice by shouting the word 'quiet!'

HEART AND LUNG FACTS

Your heart and lungs, along with their major systems (circulatory and respiratory) are amazing. Here are some facts about the organs you rely on to stay alive, healthy and active!

WORKING 24/7

You may go to sleep at night, but your body keeps on working. Your body needs nutrients and oxygen all of the time to keep your circulatory, respiratory and other systems working 24/7. So, even while you're at rest, your heart keeps pumping blood around your body and your lungs keep breathing to keep you going.

The average person takes around 16 breaths a minute, or 960 breaths an hour, or 23,040 breaths a day, or 8,409,600 breaths a year, or more than 670 million breaths in a lifetime.

After all the work it's been doing overnight, your body needs to recharge its batteries. That's why breakfast is such an important meal. It boosts your energy levels and keeps you going until lunchtime.

BLOOD AT WORK

Your blood is full of metal. The iron-rich protein haemoglobin is the substance in blood that actually carries oxygen. When it reaches your muscles, the haemoglobin releases the oxygen. At the same time, it collects waste carbon dioxide and takes it away. The picture on the right shows a computer-generated model of a haemoglobin molecule.

SELF DESTRUCT!

Body cells such as red blood cells don't live forever. They die either because they have become infected, or because they self-destruct. Once they stop working as well as they should, cells are programmed to release chemicals to break themselves apart. The bits pass out of your body as waste.

GIVING BLOOD

Healthy people can give blood to help others in need. If you give blood you should not exercise for a few hours afterwards. That's because your body needs time to build up fresh blood to replace the blood that's been taken away. Exercise would call for extra oxygen too soon. Although everyone's blood does the same job, there are four different types of blood, called 'groups'.

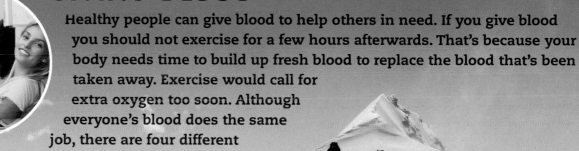

THIN AIR

High up in the mountains, the air becomes 'thinner'. That means there is less of it and it is harder to breathe. For a climber on a high mountain, each breath gives the body less oxygen than it would lower down at sea level. In response, the climber's body gradually makes more red blood cells to do a better job of capturing the available oxygen.

TESTING YOUR LIMITS

Your body is well-equipped to keep your muscles supplied with oxygen. When you exercise, your circulatory and respiratory systems start working really hard. Their job is to get oxygen to your muscles as fast as possible and to get rid of carbon dioxide and other waste quickly.

PUMP IT UP

All types of exercise call on you to be fit. Training regularly makes you fitter so you can exercise for longer. That's because using muscles often, and increasing their workload, makes them stronger. This is the basis of all training, and it works for your heart just as much as for your leg or arm muscles. When you exercise, you need to breathe harder and your heart needs to pump faster, but all that extra oxygen gets used more efficiently.

A New Zealand couple in their 60s set a world record by running a marathon (42km / 26.2 miles) every day in 2013. They finished with marathon number 366 on New Year's Day 2014!

TRAIN HIGH, RUN LOW

Athletes often get fitter by 'training high and running low'. They spend weeks training at high altitudes where the air is thinner (see page 17). Here, their bodies produce more red blood cells to capture the oxygen in the air more efficiently. Then, when they compete at lower altitudes, each breath brings in more oxygen. More oxygen plus more red blood cells means more energy – and maybe the difference between first and second place!

(see page 17)

ACTIVITY

Ask a friend to take your pulse rate and write it down. Then, jog up and down a flight of stairs three times and ask your friend to take your pulse again. You'll see that your heart has begun to work harder to get blood to your muscles.

FEEL THE BURN

People talk about 'feeling the burn' when they exercise hard. The 'burn' comes from lactic acid, which is produced as muscles use up all of the available oxygen from the blood. Hold an orange in one hand, with your arm outstretched, for a minute... or as long as you can. After a while, can you 'feel the burn'? This painful sensation is your body's way of telling you to stop whatever you are doing!

EAT, RELAX

After you've eaten a meal, your digestive system needs a lot of blood. That's why you shouldn't exercise after you've eaten. Your body finds it hard to digest food and exercise at the same time. As you exercise, your body concentrates on the muscles that are working hardest. It isn't just your heart and lungs that get to work. Your nervous system helps slow the flow of blood to other organs that don't need it urgently. It does that by narrowing the blood vessels leading there, just like squeezing shut a garden hose. At the same time, it widens the blood vessels leading to the active muscles.

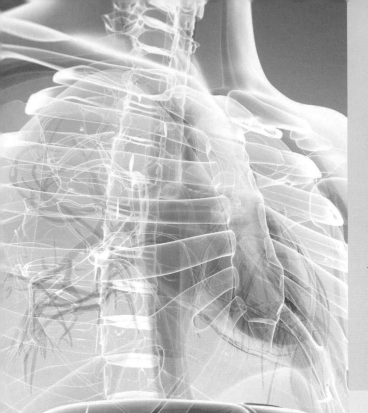

JACK OF ALL TRADES

The liver is your body's largest organ with many jobs to do. It produces proteins that give your blood the power to heal you. It filters and cleans the blood in your circulatory system. And it also helps you get the goodness out of foods that are hard to digest, such as fats.

THE BODY'S FACTORY

Your liver sits just below your diaphragm, on your right side. Like your diaphragm, lungs and heart, it's protected by your ribcage. Although it's part of your digestive system, your liver is vital to your blood and circulatory system too. It's like a factory with different departments. Some make essential substances. Others separate useful nutrients from waste in the blood. All that work uses up lots of energy. That's why there's a major vessel called the hepatic artery bringing oxygen-rich blood straight from your heart to your liver.

The liver is the only internal organ that can regenerate itself if it gets damaged. It also holds about 1/7 of your body's total blood supply at any given time!

Inferior vena cava

Aorta

Hepatic artery

Gall bladder

Portal vein

BLOOD DONATIONS

Blood arrives at the liver from two directions. Oxygen-rich blood comes through the hepatic artery directly from the aorta in your heart. The portal vein transports blood from your intestines. The oxygen in this blood has been used up in the digestive system, but at the same time it has picked up some essential nutrients. The liver filters the blood so that these nutrients can be sent out to other parts of the body.

WASTE MANAGEMENT

Your liver is made up of thousands of small features called lobules (pictured). Each lobule is connected to many vessels carrying blood to and from the liver. The lobules filter your blood. Useful nutrients are broken down and then sent back into the blood. The liver uses some of the filtered waste material to create bile, the substance that helps you digest fats. Other wastes get sent in the blood to the kidneys, which gets rid of them in your urine.

HEALING POWERS

When you cut or graze yourself, your liver helps your body to patch itself up. When your skin is damaged, special blood cells, called platelets, get to work to stop the bleeding and to create a patch – or scab – to keep germs out (as in this picture). The platelets need to combine with certain proteins called clotting factors. Clotting is a medical word to describe what happens as blood turns into a solid. These proteins are produced in your liver.

GET THE MESSAGE?

Hypothalamus

Your body sends messages to itself all the time. These chemical messages are called hormones. Some hormones produce changes over a long period, for example telling your body how to grow. Others can help you deal with sudden problems, like being chased by a vicious dog.

Thyroid gland

CHEMICAL MESSENGERS

Glands are organs in your body that produce certain types of chemicals. These chemicals have different effects in your body. Glands send off chemical hormones into your blood, so that they can reach the necessary bits of your body. Some hormones tell other organs how active they need to be – to help you digest food. Hormones also help you to deal with emergencies, giving you extra strength. Some hormones even go to other glands, to get them to make more hormones!

Thymus gland

Adrenal glands

Reproductive glands

Epinephrine is called the 'fight or flight' hormone. Your body makes it when you're in a situation where you might have to fight, or run away quickly!

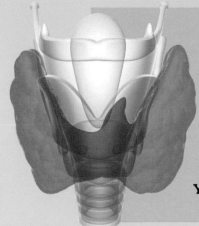

CHECK YOUR SPEED

The thyroid gland, in the front of your neck (shown here in pink), sends out a hormone to control how fast the cells in your body are using up nutrients to produce energy. That speed is called your metabolic rate. People with a high metabolic rate burn energy more quickly than those with a slower metabolic rate. The thyroid gland wraps around the front of your larynx (shown here in white). You can feel it under the skin in the front of your neck.

FEELING SLEEPY?

The pineal gland is found in your brain and is shaped like a small pine cone, which is how it got its name. This gland makes a hormone called melatonin, which regulates your sleep patterns. So when you're feeling sleepy and ready for bed, it's the pineal gland that's responsible.

LISTEN TO YOUR MASTER

Although only about the size of a pea, the pituitary gland – located at the base of your brain – is often called the 'master gland'. That's because it sends out hormones to check on other glands, making sure they work in balance with each other. Being so close to the brain helps – the pituitary gland reacts almost instantly to signals sent out by the brain.

DID YOU KNOW?

SCIENTISTS HAVE COUNTED 500 DIFFERENT FUNCTIONS CARRIED OUT BY THE LIVER

Apart from its essential roles in processing fats and filtering blood, the liver stores vitamins and minerals so that they can be put to use by your body. It even turns non-sugars such as amino acids into the glucose that your cells need to work.

EACH RED BLOOD CELL PASSES THROUGH YOUR HEART 14,000 TIMES A DAY

The main job of the red blood cells is to transport oxygen from the lungs to every part of the body. It takes about 20 seconds for blood to circulate around your entire body. The heart plays its part by constantly pushing those blood cells into the lungs to load up with oxygen, out to the body and back again... over and over again.

THE 'FIGHT OR FLIGHT' HORMONE IS YOUR LINK TO PRIMITIVE HUMANS

Epinephrene, sometimes called adrenaline, is produced when the body prepares to react to a threat or sudden stress. It causes the heart to beat faster and the airways into the lungs to widen. These reactions boost your strength so that you can take on an attacking wolf or run away from armed warriors. You might also notice its effects when you have a test at school.

YOUR BODY

PRODUCES 2.4 MILLION
NEW RED BLOOD CELLS
EVERY SECOND

And about a billion of those cells can be found in just a few drops of blood. These blood cells remain 'in circulation' for about 100 days before your body recycles them. Blood banks can freeze and store red blood cells for up to ten years, but once they've been thawed they need to be used within 24 hours.

ABOUT 1 LITRE
(2 PINTS) OF AIR ALWAYS STAYS IN YOUR LUNGS,
NO MATTER HOW HARD YOU
BREATHE OUT

It's meant to stay there, because it allows the alveoli and other airways in your lungs to remain open (like tiny balloons). This means that receiving oxygen and getting rid of carbon dioxide and other wastes continues the whole time.

FREQUENTLY ASKED QUESTIONS

WHAT'S THE WORLD RECORD FOR HOLDING YOUR BREATH UNDERWATER?

The record for taking a deep breath of air and holding it for as long as possible is 11 minutes, 54 seconds. It was set by Stephane Mifsud of France, in June 2009. Breathing in pure oxygen, rather than air, for up to 30 minutes beforehand allows trained divers to last almost twice as long. That's why the record after breathing pure oxygen is 23 minutes and 1 second, set by Goran Colak of Croatia in June 2014.

WHY DOES YOUR VOICE SOUND SQUEAKY WHEN YOU BREATHE IN HELIUM GAS FROM A BALLOON?

In fact, the pitch of the voice (whether a note is higher or lower) doesn't really change. That funny sound comes from a different feature called 'timbre'. Think of the same note played by a trumpet and a violin: the two notes are at the same pitch but they sound different because they have different timbres. Helium is less dense than air, so it passes through your larynx, or voicebox, faster than air, changing the timbre of your voice.

WHAT HAPPENS TO YOUR HORMONES WHILE YOU ARE ASLEEP?

Sleep is a very important time for the body to carry out lots of jobs so that you wake up in the morning feeling refreshed and alert. As you sleep, growth hormones are released. These are essential for normal growth and development, and they also get to work to repair and maintain muscles and bones. In fact, all your body tissues are renewed more quickly while you are asleep than when you are awake. Your body also controls feelings of hunger by balancing two different hormones while you are sleeping. Not getting enough sleep can upset this balance and cause people to eat too much.

WHY DOES BEING OVERWEIGHT INCREASE THE RISK OF HEART DISEASE?

Your heart is a muscle, and a lot of heart disease is caused by forcing that muscle to work too hard. The body has to make nearly 25 km (15 miles) of blood vessels for each kilo (2.2 pounds) of fat that a person gains. So the heart has to work much harder to pump blood through all that extra distance.

SYSTEMS OF THE BODY

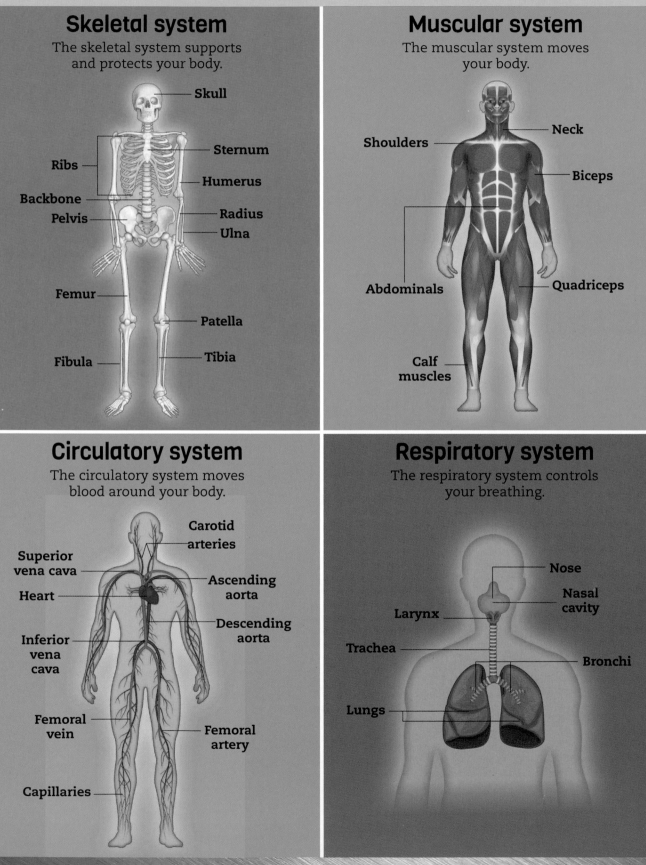

Skeletal system

The skeletal system supports and protects your body.

- Skull
- Sternum
- Ribs
- Humerus
- Backbone
- Pelvis
- Radius
- Ulna
- Femur
- Patella
- Fibula
- Tibia

Muscular system

The muscular system moves your body.

- Neck
- Shoulders
- Biceps
- Abdominals
- Quadriceps
- Calf muscles

Circulatory system

The circulatory system moves blood around your body.

- Carotid arteries
- Superior vena cava
- Ascending aorta
- Heart
- Descending aorta
- Inferior vena cava
- Femoral vein
- Femoral artery
- Capillaries

Respiratory system

The respiratory system controls your breathing.

- Nose
- Nasal cavity
- Larynx
- Trachea
- Bronchi
- Lungs

This is your quick reference guide to the main systems of the body: skeletal, muscular, respiratory, circulatory, digestive, nervous, endocrine and lymphatic.

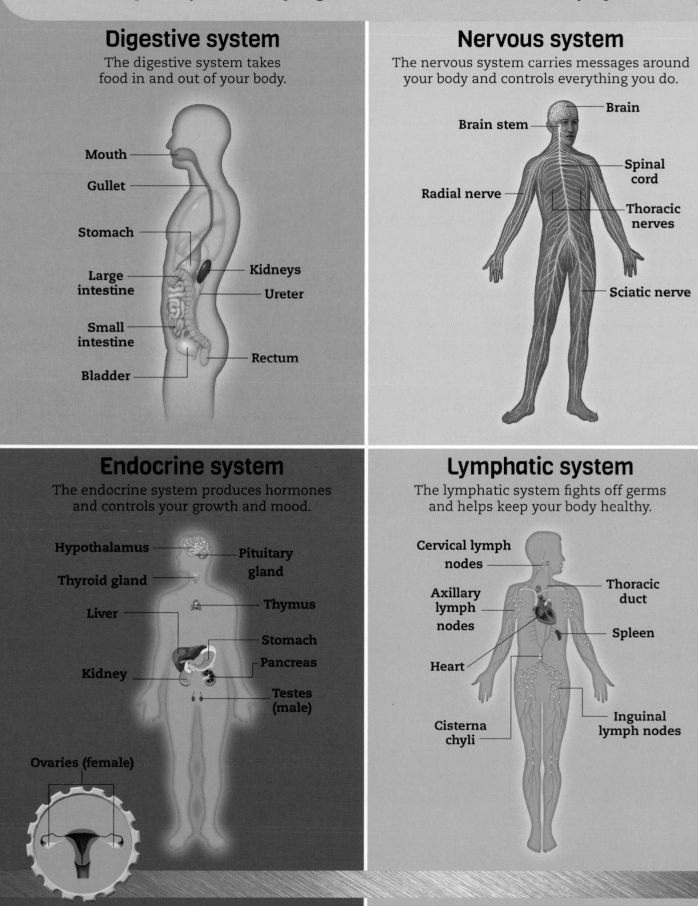

Digestive system
The digestive system takes food in and out of your body.

- Mouth
- Gullet
- Stomach
- Large intestine
- Kidneys
- Ureter
- Small intestine
- Rectum
- Bladder

Nervous system
The nervous system carries messages around your body and controls everything you do.

- Brain
- Brain stem
- Spinal cord
- Radial nerve
- Thoracic nerves
- Sciatic nerve

Endocrine system
The endocrine system produces hormones and controls your growth and mood.

- Hypothalamus
- Pituitary gland
- Thyroid gland
- Liver
- Thymus
- Stomach
- Pancreas
- Kidney
- Testes (male)
- Ovaries (female)

Lymphatic system
The lymphatic system fights off germs and helps keep your body healthy.

- Cervical lymph nodes
- Axillary lymph nodes
- Thoracic duct
- Spleen
- Heart
- Cisterna chyli
- Inguinal lymph nodes

GLOSSARY

alveolus One of the tiny air sacs in the lungs.

amino acid An essential nutrient containing several chemical elements.

aorta The main artery in the body, which carries oxygenated blood away from the heart.

artery One of the main vessels carrying blood from the heart to other parts of the body.

atrium One of the two chambers in which blood enters the heart.

bronchiole One of the smaller tubes that branch off the bronchi and carry air to the alveoli in the lungs.

bronchus One of the two main tubes that carries air into the lungs.

capillary One of the smallest of the body's blood vessels.

circulatory system Made up of the heart, blood vessels and blood, this system transports oxygen, carbon dioxide, nutrients, hormones and blood cells to and from cells around your body. The blood is pumped by the heart and transported in the arteries and veins.

diaphragm The large muscle beneath the lungs that controls breathing.

digestion The process of breaking down food in the body to release essential nutrients.

gland An organ that produces and stores hormones for release into the body.

hormone A chemical that helps to regulate processes such as reproduction and growth.

intestines The large and small intestines are the part of the digestive system where nutrients are released from the food into the bloodstream.

larynx (voicebox) The organ in the neck that holds the vocal cords, responsible for producing the voice. It is part of the respiratory system.

liver A major organ in the digestive system which has many jobs including filtering the blood coming from the digestive system.

metabolism The chemical processes that the body's cells use to produce energy from food, get rid of waste and heal themselves.

mineral A chemical substance, such as iron, which is important for health but which the body cannot produce.

nutrient Any substance that the body needs for energy or growth.

plasma The fluid that carries the different blood cells through the body.

platelet A blood cell that helps healing by binding with other platelets when they detect a damaged blood vessel. When platelets dry, they form a scab.

protein One of the most important of all molecules in the body, protein is needed to strengthen and replace tissue in the body.

pulmonary circulation The movement of blood between the heart and the lungs.

pulse The regular beat felt in the wrist or the neck as the heart pumps blood around the body.

respiratory system The organs and tissues that allow you to breathe.

trachea (windpipe) The tube that connects the pharynx and larynx to the lungs.

urine The liquid waste filtered by your kidneys, taken to the bladder along the ureters.

vein One of the main vessels carrying blood from different parts of the body to the heart.

ventricle One of the two chambers from which blood leaves the heart.

vocal cords The two pairs of membranes in the larynx.

FURTHER READING

Body Works by Anna Claybourne (QED Publishing, 2014)

Complete Book of the Human Body by Anna Claybourne (Usborne Books, 2013)

Everything You Need to Know about the Human Body by Patricia MacNair (Kingfisher, 2011)

Horrible Science: Body Owner's Handbook by Nick Arnold (Scholastic Press, 2014)

Mind Webs: Human Body by Anna Claybourne (Wayland, 2014)

Project Science: Human Body by Sally Hewitt (Franklin Watts, 2012)

INDEX

A
adrenal glands 22
alveoli 12, 13, 25
aorta 7, 8, 21
arteries 6, 7, 8, 9, 11, 20, 21

B
bile 21
blood banks 25
blood clotting 21
blood groups 17
breathing 5, 10, 12–13, 14,
    16, 17, 18, 19, 25, 26
bronchi 12, 13
bronchioles 12, 13

C
capillaries 9, 13
carbon dioxide 9, 13, 14, 17,
    18, 25
cilia 12
circulatory system 8–9, 16,
    18, 20

D
diaphragm 14, 20
digestion 19, 20, 21, 22

E
energy 10, 12, 16, 19, 20, 23
epinephrine 22, 24
exercise 5, 10, 11, 15, 17, 18–19

F
fats 20, 21, 24, 27
'fight or flight' 5, 22, 24
fitness 10-11, 18-19

G
glands 22–3

H
haemoglobin 17

heart 4, 5, 6–7, 8, 10–11, 16,
    20, 24
heartbeat 5, 6–7, 10
hormones 22–3, 27
hypothalamus 22

I
infection 9
iron 17

K
kidneys 21

L
lactic acid 19
larynx (voicebox) 15, 23, 26
lips 15
liver 20–1, 24
lungs 4, 5, 6, 7, 9, 12–13, 14,
    15, 16, 19, 20, 24, 25

M
melatonin 23
metabolic rate 23
muscles 10, 14, 17, 18–19, 27

N
nervous system 19
nutrients 8, 9, 11, 16, 20, 23

O
oxygen 4, 6, 8, 9, 10, 12, 13,
    16, 17, 18, 19, 20, 21, 26

P
pineal gland 23
pituitary gland 23
plasma 9
platelets 9, 21
proteins 20, 21
pulmonary circulation
    13
pulse 6, 19

R
red blood cells 9, 17, 19, 25
respiratory system 12–13,
    14, 16, 18
ribs 6, 14

S
scabs 9, 21
sleep 4, 16, 23, 27
smoking 11
speaking 14-15

T
teeth 15
thymus gland 22
thyroid gland 22, 23
tongue 15
trachea (windpipe) 12, 15

U
urine 21

V
veins 7, 8, 9, 13, 21
ventricles 7, 8
vitamins 9, 24
vocal cords 15
voice 26

W
white blood cells 9

BODYWORKS

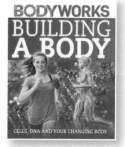

BUILDING A BODY
• Building a Body • All in the Mix • Body Builder • Back to Basics • Small Beginnings • Brand New You • Growing Up • You Are Unique • A Code for Life • All Part of the Family • Did You Know? • Frequently Asked Questions • Systems of the Body

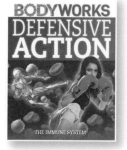

DEFENSIVE ACTION
• Defensive Action • Germ Warfare • Rapid Response • Fighting Back • Lymphatic System • Temperature Control • Super Organs • Teamwork • Injury Time • Outside Help • Did You Know? • Frequently Asked Questions • Systems of the Body

FUELLING THE BODY
• Fuelling the Body • Open Wide • Down the Hatch • Stomach Churning • Big and Small • A Balanced Diet • Helpful Allies • Blood Cleaning • The Power Station • An Active You! • Did You Know? • Frequently Asked Questions • Systems of the Body

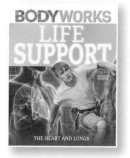

LIFE SUPPORT
• Life Support • Have a Heart • Round and Round • Take Care of Your Heart • A Breath of Fresh Air • Speak Out! • Heart and Lung Facts • Testing Your Limits • Jack of All Trades • Get the Message? • Did You Know? • Frequently Asked Questions • Systems of the Body

READY FOR ACTION
• Ready for Action • The Skeleton Crew • The Hard Stuff • Meat on the Bones • Muscle Power • Working Non-Stop • Tying It All Together • Skin Deep • Tough as Nails • Spare Parts? • Did You Know? • Frequently Asked Questions • Systems of the Body

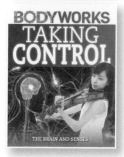

TAKING CONTROL
• Taking Control • The Brain Is Boss • What a Nerve! • Eye Spy • Hear, Hear! • Smells Good, Tastes Great • How Touching • Changing Your Mind • Behind the Scenes • Your Personal Computer? • Did You Know? • Frequently Asked Questions • Systems of the Body